Pass the GED™

Language Arts, **Writing Test**

4

5 STEPS TO TEST SUCCESS

New Readers Press

Contents

Copyright © 2003 by Trian Publishing Company
Distributed by
  New Readers Press
  Division of ProLiteracy Worldwide
  1320 Jamesville Avenue, Syracuse, New York 13210
  www.newreaderspress.com

Pass the GED™ Writng Team
Project Developer: Caren Van Slyke
Writer: Karin Evans
Editor: Pam Bliss
Project Manager: Mark Ondrla
Copy Editor: Louise Howe
Production Manager: Jean Farley Brown
Cover Design and Illustrator: Karen Blanchard

Printed in the United States of America
9 8 7 6 5 4 3
ISBN: 978-1-56420-479-0

Five Steps to Test Success

You have been preparing for the GED Writing Test by practicing essay writing and by reviewing key topics in grammar, sentence structure, spelling, punctuation, and capitalization.

As you get closer to taking the GED, it makes sense to ask, "What are the best steps I can take to make sure that I pass the GED Writing Test?" That's where this book comes in. This book doesn't teach you to write—it teaches you about the GED Writing Test. *Pass the GED™ Language Arts, Writing Test* is an invaluable companion to your other GED study materials, but—unlike those other books, videos, or software—its only job is to help you figure out how to apply your knowledge and skills to passing the test.

This book takes you through the **Five Steps to GED Test Success:**

Step 1: Know What To Expect on the Test

Get clear on such basic issues as how many questions are on the test and how long you have to answer them. Find out key information that will help you write a strong essay.

Step 2: Practice Different Types of GED Questions

Questions on the GED Writing Test are different from the types you may remember from school, such as, "What is the subject of the sentence?" On Part I of the test, you will answer multiple-choice questions based on passages that need correction and improvement. You will learn how to work with the four types of questions that you will encounter on Part I of the GED Writing Test.

Step 3: Prepare for the Essay

To pass the GED, you need to write a good essay on the topic that is provided to you. In this section you will learn strategies for planning, writing, and polishing your essay in 45 minutes. In the back of this book, you can see the scoring guide that will be used to evaluate your essay.

Step 4: Practice Taking the GED

There's nothing like the real thing. This section will help you ease in with some *Practice Test Warm-Ups.* Then you will take a full-length *Practice GED Language Arts, Writing Test.* You will answer similar questions to the ones you will see on the test, working under the same time limit you'll have when you take the GED.

Step 5: Make Your Plan to Pass the Test

At the end of the book, you will have a chance to make a plan based on all that you have learned about the GED and about yourself. You and your teacher may determine that you are ready to take the GED Writing Test, or you may see that you need to develop your skills a little more. Use the *GED Personal Coach™* on pages 38–39 to help you make your final plan.

Besides providing you with lots of test advice and practice, this book will occasionally ask you to STOP AND THINK. We will ask you to explain why you chose a particular answer to a question. We will ask you to think about how you are doing and how you can improve. Make the most of these opportunities, and you will see that your test performance will increase dramatically! Now, on to Step 1…

Frequently Asked Questions About the GED Language Arts, Writing Test

Q: **How many questions are on the GED Writing Test? How long do I have to answer them?**

A: There are 50 questions on Part I of the GED Language Arts, Writing Test. You will have to read six or seven passages (similar to the ones in this book) and answer from five to eight multiple-choice questions based on each passage. You will have 75 minutes to complete this part of the test before you start the essay.

The questions in Part I test your ability to spot and correct errors as well as to improve the clarity of sentences and organization of paragraphs. Always read each passage carefully, looking for errors and problems to fix. Then read and answer each question based on the passage.

Q: **Isn't there also an essay?**

A: Yes! Part II is an essay. The essay is based on a topic that adults can write about, based on their own personal experiences. Don't worry that you need special knowledge to write the essay or that the topic will be too difficult. The topic, which is called the "prompt" in the scoring guide (see page 44), will be several sentences long. It may contain a direct question for you to answer, or it may state a general idea and ask you to explain or discuss that idea in some way.

Q: **Is there enough time to write a passing essay?**

A: You will have 45 minutes to plan and write your essay. That may sound tough, but students who have taken the GED report that it is enough time to plan and write an essay that is well organized with supporting facts and details.

You should take 5 or 10 minutes to plan your essay on scratch paper before you write your draft. You will have an answer sheet with lines to write the essay on. After you write your draft, you can read it over and make changes, additions, and corrections neatly on your answer sheet. The people who are scoring your essay know that this is your first draft and that you didn't have time to revise it. They keep that in mind when they score your work.

You will have a chance to practice planning and writing an essay in 45 minutes on page 37.

Q: **How will my essay be scored?**

A: Your essay will be read fairly quickly by two trained readers. The readers won't be looking for a particular answer, and they won't mark on your paper. Instead, they want to get an overall impression of your writing. This is called "holistic scoring" because it treats your writing as a whole rather than focusing on particular characteristics.

Each reader will give your essay a score on the following scale:
4—effective
3—adequate
2—marginal
1—inadequate

Your essay score will be the average of the two readers' scores.

Q: What score do I need to pass the Writing Test?

A: You need two scores to pass the GED. You will need a PASSING score of <u>at least</u> 410* on each test and an AVERAGE score of <u>at least</u> 450* for all five tests. For example, if you get an essay score of 2 (out of 4), you need to get about 40 multiple-choice questions correct to earn a score of 450. You should try to get as many questions correct as possible. Because you need an average of 450 for <u>all five tests</u>, you will need "above average" scores on some tests to balance possible "below average" scores on others.

IMPORTANT NOTE: No matter how many multiple-choice questions you get right on Part I, you CANNOT pass the GED Writing Test unless you get an essay score of 2 or higher. It's a rule.

Q: Back to Part I. What do I need to know to pass the multiple-choice part of the test?

A: The questions are based on four major categories of writing knowledge and skills:
- **Sentence Structure** 30%
  Correct fragments, run-on sentences, and comma splices; use conjunctions and clauses to combine sentences effectively; correct errors in parallel structure and in modifiers.
- **Usage** 30%
  Correct errors in subject-verb agreement, verb form and tense, and pronoun reference.
- **Mechanics** 25%
  Correct errors in capitalization, commas, and spelling. The only spelling errors tested are related to homonyms, possessives, and contractions.
- **Organization** 15%
  Combine and divide paragraphs, identify an effective topic sentence, reorder sentences, remove an irrelevant sentence.

Q: What can I do to pass the test?

A: Follow a study plan developed by you and your teacher. Use this book to help you be certain you are really ready for the test. Practice your writing as often as possible by keeping a journal and writing practice essays. Write letters or e-mail messages to friends and family members. Stay in the habit of writing frequently so that you are used to putting your thoughts into words. Also, read as much as you can, even everyday materials such as letters and memos, advertising, and magazine articles. See if you notice any errors—and think about how you would correct them! The questions on the GED Writing Test are based on just these sorts of everyday materials.

* These numbers are minimum scores set by the GED Testing Service. States, provinces, and territories may set higher scores. Check with your teacher or the state Department of Adult Education to determine your requirements.

Your Turn

What other questions do you have about the GED Writing Test? Write them here and discuss them with your teacher.

_____

_____

_____

_____

Correction Questions

On Part I of the GED Writing Test, you'll see different types of multiple-choice questions. One type is called correction. A **correction question** asks which correction should be made to a sentence or pair of sentences. It is followed by five choices. Sometimes the fifth choice is "no correction is necessary." Many different kinds of errors are tested by this type of question.

EXAMPLE

(1) Most people have very little privacy at work. (2) Contemporary offices have open work areas and cubicles. (3) Workers in production and manufacturing jobs don't even have desks to call there own.

1. Sentence 3: **Workers in production and manufacturing jobs don't even have desks to call there own.**

   Which correction should be made to sentence 3?

   (1) insert a comma after <u>Workers</u>
   (2) insert a comma after <u>jobs</u>
   (3) change <u>don't</u> to <u>doesn't</u>
   (4) replace <u>there</u> with <u>their</u>
   (5) no correction is necessary

Answer and Explanations

The answer choices cover several different areas of content. If you cannot identify an error in the sentence, try testing each answer choice to see if it seems to make the sentence correct.

The correct answer is **(4) replace <u>there</u> with <u>their</u>.**
The words *there, their,* and *they're* are commonly confused. In this sentence, the possessive pronoun *their* is needed to show the sense of ownership. The word *there* means "in that place."

Choices (1) and (2) insert unnecessary commas, which would be errors. Choice (3) creates an error in subject-verb agreement.

Try It Yourself

(4) When you are on the job you should protect your privacy. (5) Many people who bring their personal business into the workplace come to regret it later.

2. Sentence 4: **When you are on the job you should protect your privacy.**

   Which correction should be made to sentence 4?

   (1) replace <u>When</u> with <u>Although</u>
   (2) replace <u>you are</u> with <u>one is</u>
   (3) change <u>are</u> to <u>were</u>
   (4) insert a comma after <u>job</u>
   (5) replace <u>your</u> with <u>you're</u>

Think It Through

Which do you think is the correct answer?

The correct answer is _____

Why do you think this is the correct answer? Give a specific reason.

_____

_____

_____

Answer and Explanation: The correct answer is **(4) insert a comma after <u>job</u>.** This sentence begins with a dependent clause, which needs a comma after it. Choice (1) doesn't show the correct relationship between being on the job and protecting your privacy. Choice (2) makes the pronouns in the sentence shift from *one* to *you.* Choice (3) mistakenly uses the past tense in part of the sentence. Choice (5) substitutes the contraction of *you are,* which would not make sense.

Practice

Choose the one best answer to each question below. Write short explanations for your answers to questions 1 and 2.

Questions 1 and 2 are based on the paragraph below.

(1) The KC Women's Shelter has developed a new program in a key area of need. (2) The shelter now pares our clients with volunteers who have skills in career development. (3) Our clients often are qualified for various types of jobs. (4) Even so they often need support for conducting a job search.

1. Sentence 2: **The shelter now pares our clients with volunteers who have skills in career development.**

   Which correction should be made to sentence 2?

   (1) change <u>shelter</u> to <u>Shelter</u>
   (2) replace <u>pares</u> with <u>pairs</u>
   (3) insert a comma after <u>clients</u>
   (4) change <u>have</u> to <u>had</u>
   (5) insert a comma after <u>skills</u>

   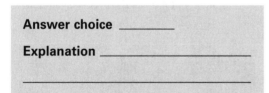

   Answer choice _____

   Explanation _____

   _____

2. Sentence 4: **Even so they often need support for conducting a job search.**

   Which correction should be made to sentence 4?

   (1) insert a comma after <u>so</u>
   (2) change <u>they</u> to <u>them</u>
   (3) change <u>need</u> to <u>needs</u>
   (4) insert a comma after <u>support</u>
   (5) no correction is necessary

   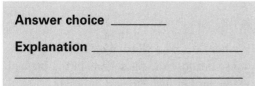

   Answer choice _____

   Explanation _____

   _____

Questions 3 and 4 are based on the e-mail message below.

To: All Front Desk Workers

(1) Effective May 1, our business hours will be 8 A.M. to 8 P.M. (2) The company is making this change in response to our customers' many requests to reach us after 5 P.M. (3) I'm writing to ask your help in covering the phones! (4) Please reply to this e-mail, indicate whether you can work a regular 5 to 8 P.M. shift at least once per week.

3. Sentence 2: **The company is making this change in response to our customers' many requests to reach us after 5 P.M.**

   Which correction should be made to sentence 2?

   (1) change <u>company</u> to <u>Company</u>
   (2) change <u>is</u> to <u>are</u>
   (3) insert a comma after <u>change</u>
   (4) change <u>us</u> to <u>you</u>
   (5) no correction is necessary

4. Sentence 4: **Please reply to this e-mail, indicate whether you can work a regular 5 to 8 P.M. shift at least once per week.**

   Which correction should be made to sentence 4?

   (1) change <u>Please</u> to <u>If you please</u>
   (2) insert <u>and</u> before <u>indicate</u>
   (3) replace <u>you</u> with <u>one</u>
   (4) insert a comma after <u>shift</u>
   (5) no correction is necessary

   Check answers and explanations on page 40.

STEP 2

Revision Questions

A GED **revision question** asks you to focus on a specific, underlined part of a sentence or pair of sentences. The answer choices consist of different ways to rewrite the underlined portion. Be aware of one unusual format for revision questions. If the original sentence is correct, choose option (1), which is always the same as the original.

(1) If your produce drawer is full of aging, rubbery vegetables. (2) It's time to make soup. (3) Start by chopping and frying an onion and some fresh garlic in olive oil.

1. Sentences 1 and 2: **If your produce drawer is full of aging, rubbery <u>vegetables. It's</u> time to make soup.**

   Which is the best way to write the underlined portion of these sentences? If the original is the best way, choose option (1).

   (1) vegetables. It's
   (2) vegetables it's
   (3) vegetables, it's
   (4) vegetables, and it's
   (5) vegetables then it's

Answer and Explanations

Although there may be several ways to fix the error in the original pair of sentences, only one correct way will be listed. If you are not sure what is wrong in the original sentence, try replacing the underlined part with each of the answer choices to see which one seems to improve the sentence.

The correct answer is **(3) vegetables, its.** Sentence 1 is a fragment. Choice (3) connects it to the sentence that follows by making it an introductory dependent clause.

Choice (2) lacks the comma needed after the introductory clause. Choice (4) connects the fragment, but the word *and* is unnecessary and even confusing. Choice (5) connects the fragment, but it lacks the necessary comma.

Try It Yourself

(4) Next add some canned or homemade soup stock to the onion and garlic. (5) While the stock heating up, chop your elderly veggies. (6) Add them to the stock gradually.

2. Sentence 5: **While the stock <u>heating</u> up, chop your elderly veggies.**

   Which is the best way to write the underlined portion of this sentence? If the original is the best way, choose option (1).

   (1) heating
   (2) is heating
   (3) heated
   (4) are heating
   (5) will be heating

Think It Through

Which do you think is the correct answer?

The correct answer is _____

Why do you think this is the correct answer? Give a specific reason.

_____

_____

_____

Answer and Explanation: The correct answer is **(2) is heating.** The word *heating* is not a complete verb. Choices (3) and (5) are in the wrong tense because the passage is in the present tense. Choice (4) contains an error in subject-verb agreement because *stock* is singular.

Practice

Choose the <u>one best answer</u> to each question. Write explanations for questions 1 and 2.

<u>Questions 1 and 2</u> are based on the paragraph below.

(1) Contractors who need day laborers for temporary work often drive to home center superstores to recruit workers. (2) Men who want work pouring concrete, painting, or putting up drywall hanging out near the stores. (3) This system has certain advantages it also creates safety risks.

1. Sentence 2: **Men who want work pouring concrete, painting, or putting up <u>drywall hanging</u> out near the stores.**

   Which is the best way to write the underlined portion? If the original is the best way, choose option (1).

   (1) drywall hanging
   (2) drywall, hanging
   (3) drywall hangs
   (4) drywall, hang
   (5) drywall hang

   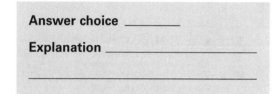

   Answer choice _____

   Explanation _____

   _____

2. Sentence 3: **This system has certain <u>advantages it</u> also creates safety risks.**

   Which is the best way to write the underlined portion? If the original is the best way, choose option (1).

   (1) advantages it
   (2) advantages, it
   (3) advantages, but it
   (4) advantages, for it
   (5) advantages, so it

   Answer choice _____

   Explanation _____

   _____

<u>Questions 3 and 4</u> are based on the letter below.

Dear Mr. Karlowski:

(1) Thank you for your letter explaining why you plan to break your lease. (2) We are aware that recent construction projects in the area had caused problems for commercial tenants. (3) We value our relationship with you and have preferred not to lose you as a tenant. (4) Before making a final decision, please meet with us in person. (5) Perhaps we can come to an agreement that will benefit us all.

3. Sentence 2: **We are aware that recent construction projects in the area <u>had caused</u> problems for commercial tenants.**

   Which is the best way to write the underlined portion of this sentence? If the original is the best way, choose option (1).

   (1) had caused
   (2) will have caused
   (3) has caused
   (4) have caused
   (5) had been causing

4. Sentence 3: **We value our relationship with you and <u>have preferred</u> not to lose you as a tenant.**

   Which is the best way to write the underlined portion of this sentence? If the original is the best way, choose option (1).

   (1) have preferred
   (2) prefers
   (3) prefer
   (4) preferring
   (5) preferred

Check answers and explanations on page 40.

STEP 2

Construction Shift Questions

To answer a GED **construction shift question,** you need to figure out how to rewrite a sentence or combine two sentences. These questions are not based on errors but rather on opportunities to improve text that is wordy, unclear, awkward-sounding, or repetitive. You will need to rearrange the words in your head—keeping necessary words but dropping unnecessary ones. This is similar to revising your own writing, but the multiple-choice format makes it a little trickier.

EXAMPLE

1. Sentences 1 and 2: **Next time your car is involved in an accident, your insurance company might send you to its own facility. This facility would handle your vehicle inspection, rental car, and repairs.**

   The most effective combination of sentences 1 and 2 would include which group of words?

   (1) facility, this facility would handle
   (2) facility, which would handle
   (3) its own facility would handle
   (4) sending you for vehicle inspection
   (5) its own facility, being one to handle

Answer and Explanations

There is no error in sentences 1 and 2, but they can be smoothly combined. The key to combining them is noticing that the word *facility* is repeated.

The correct answer is **(2) facility, which would handle.** The complete sentence would read, *Next time your car is involved in an accident, your insurance company might send you to its own facility, which would handle your vehicle inspection, rental car, and repairs.*

You can test the other answer choices by trying to see if you can create a clear, correct sentence with them. You'll have a hard time!

Try It Yourself

2. Sentence 3: **Critics of these insurance facilities worry about them because they are concerned that insurance companies will save money on repair costs by using cheaper parts and cutting corners.**

   If you rewrote sentence 3 beginning with

   <u>Critics of these insurance facilities worry that</u>

   the next words should be

   (1) insurance companies
   (2) they are concerned
   (3) saving money
   (4) repair costs
   (5) using cheaper parts

Think It Through

Which do you think is the correct answer?

The correct answer is _____

Why do you think this is the correct answer? Give a specific reason.

_____

_____

_____

Answer and Explanation: The correct answer is **(1) insurance companies.** The new sentence would read, *Critics of these insurance facilities worry that insurance companies will save money on repair costs by using cheaper parts and cutting corners.* The new sentence is less wordy. If you try the other choices, you will find it difficult to keep the meaning of the original sentence.

Practice

Choose the <u>one best answer</u> to each question. Write explanations for questions 1 and 2.

<u>Questions 1 and 2</u> are based on the paragraph below.

(1) Different people have different needs in the case of trying to concentrate on challenging work. (2) Some people need activity around them. (3) The buzz of activity helps them focus, so they work well in an area near others.

1. Sentence 1: **Different people have different needs in the case of trying to concentrate on challenging work.**

   The most effective revision of sentence 1 would include which group of words?

   (1) In trying to be different
   (2) in challenging themselves
   (3) Differently trying to concentrate
   (4) needs, however, to concentrate
   (5) needs when they are trying to

   > **Answer choice** _____
   >
   > **Explanation** _____
   >
   > _____

2. Sentences 2 and 3: **Some people need activity around them. The buzz of activity helps them focus, so they work well in an area near others.**

   The most effective combination of sentences 2 and 3 would include which group of words?

   (1) need the buzz of activity to focus,
   (2) around them the activity buzzes
   (3) Although some people need
   (4) people working well in an open area
   (5) people needing a buzz of activity

   > **Answer choice** _____
   >
   > **Explanation** _____
   >
   > _____

<u>Questions 3 and 4</u> are based on the memo.

To all singers:
(1) Please prepare for our concert by warming up your voice at home. (2) You should also review your music. (3) When you enter the concert hall, please be quiet as it will be the time the musicians are tuning their instruments.

3. Sentences 1 and 2: **Please prepare for our concert by warming up your voice at home. You should also review your music.**

   Which is the most effective combination of sentences 1 and 2?

   (1) Please prepare for our concert by warming up your voice at home, and you should review your music.
   (2) Please prepare for our concert by warming up your voice at home, also reviewing your music.
   (3) Please prepare for our concert, warming up your voice at home and also review your music.
   (4) Please prepare for our concert by warming up your voice at home and reviewing your music.
   (5) Please prepare for our concert by warming up your voice at home, while also reviewing your music.

4. Sentence 3: **When you enter the concert hall, please be quiet as it will be the time the musicians are tuning their instruments.**

   The most effective revision of sentence 3 would include which groups of words?

   (1) entering the concert hall
   (2) The concert hall must be entered
   (3) quiet because the musicians will be tuning
   (4) the musicians will be quiet
   (5) as you are quietly warming up

   Check answers and explanations on page 40.

Organization Questions

GED **organization questions** ask you to improve a paragraph or a passage. You may choose topic sentences, correctly order sentences in a paragraph, divide one paragraph into two paragraphs, combine two paragraphs into one, or eliminate irrelevant ideas from paragraphs.

Sample Passage

(A)

(1) Now that people live longer and stay healthier, they tend to extend their working lives. (2) Look around at the "retirement-age" of people you know. (3) Chances are that few of them are retired! (4) Young people now tend to plan their lives differently also.

(B)

(5) One new trend is that older people are more likely to start businesses of their own. (6) They give a variety of reasons for taking on these risky ventures.

(C)

(7) Many older people feel that they do not have enough retirement savings. (8) Others want to help their families by employing their children and other family members.

E X A M P L E

1. Which revision would improve the effectiveness of paragraph A?

(1) remove sentence 1
(2) move sentence 3 to follow sentence 4
(3) move sentence 4 to follow sentence 1
(4) remove sentence 4
(5) no revision is necessary

Answer and Explanations

Ask yourself; *Do all the sentences relate to the main idea? Are they in logical order?*

The correct answer is **(4) remove sentence 4.** Sentence 4 is not closely related to the topic. Removing it improves the paragraph.

Choice (1) removes the topic sentence. Choices (2) and (3) reorder sentences, making the paragraph even harder to read.

Try It Yourself

2. Which revision would improve the effectiveness of the article?

(1) join paragraphs A and B
(2) join paragraphs B and C
(3) move paragraph B to follow paragraph C
(4) remove paragraph B
(5) remove paragraph C

Think It Through

Which do you think is the correct answer?

The correct answer is _____

Why do you think this is the correct answer? Give a specific reason.

_____

_____

Answer and Explanation: The correct answer is **(2) join paragraphs B and C.** Paragraph C gives reasons that older people start new businesses, so it helps explain the main idea of paragraph B. You wouldn't join paragraphs A and B—Choice (1)—because B starts a new idea. C elaborates on B, so you wouldn't change their order, as suggested by Choice (3). There is no reason to remove either paragraph—Choices (4) and (5)—since they both relate to the topic.

Practice

Choose the <u>one best answer</u> to each question. Write explanations for questions 1 and 2.

<u>Questions 1 and 2</u> are based on the article below.

(1) People should know when the seasons turn cold or warm. (2) However, most people act as if they have no idea that the weather changes. (3) Ask any heating company how many furnaces get checked *before* it turns cold. (4) Or ask any air conditioning repairer what happens during the year's first heat wave. (5) If you are responsible for any weather-related building systems, do yourself a favor. (6) Make an annual schedule for your maintenance calls. (7) You'll find that many "emergency" service calls are preventable.

1. Which revision would improve the effectiveness of the article?

    Begin a new paragraph with

    (1) sentence 3
    (2) sentence 4
    (3) sentence 5
    (4) sentence 6
    (5) sentence 7

    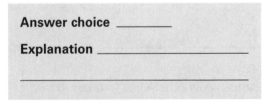

    Answer choice _____

    Explanation _____

    _____

2. Which revision should be made to the placement of sentence 6?

    (1) remove sentence 6
    (2) move sentence 6 to follow sentence 1
    (3) move sentence 6 to follow sentence 7
    (4) begin the article with sentence 6
    (5) no revision is necessary

    Answer choice _____

    Explanation _____

    _____

<u>Questions 3 and 4</u> are based on the business document below.

(A)
(1) In this tight economy, our sales remain slow. (2) However, Romar Motors remains committed to keeping our employees fully employed through this difficult period. (3) We ask everyone to have realistic expectations for raises in the employee review period. (4) We will be offering the same health insurance.

(B)
(5) We've got a raise policy. (6) It will be given to all department heads. (7) The policy also will be available for everyone to read, from executives to garage workers.

(C)
(8) At the same time, we will make every effort to show our appreciation to our employees in less costly ways. (9) Please call or e-mail Thea Perkins with any suggestions you have for recognizing our people's contributions.

3. Which revision would improve the effectiveness of paragraph A?

    (1) remove sentence 2
    (2) remove sentence 4
    (3) move sentence 4 to follow sentence 1
    (4) move sentence 4 to follow sentence 2
    (5) no revision is necessary

4. Which is the most effective rewrite of sentence 5?

    (1) A clear, fair raise policy will be followed at every level.
    (2) Here is what you should know about our raise policy.
    (3) A raise policy tells who gets what kind of raise and when.
    (4) Even the garage workers need to know the policy on raises.
    (5) Every company needs a raise policy.

Check answers and explanations on page 40.

Respond to the Topic

You will have 45 minutes to write an essay in response to a **topic.** Your essay score will depend partly on how well you stick to the topic. First, read the topic carefully. Think about what it is asking. Next, develop a **focus statement,** a main point about the topic on which you can base your essay. Then pinpoint how you will support your focus statement. This step will take a few minutes, but it will help you stick to the topic as you write—and help you get a high score.

EXAMPLE

TOPIC A

The saying "Every cloud has a silver lining" means that every bad thing has a good side.

In your experience, is this idea true? Use your personal observations, experience, and knowledge to support your answer.

Read and think: What is the topic asking?
Do I think it's true that every bad thing has a good side, based on my own experiences?

Write a focus statement: What will be my main point?
I believe it's true that every bad thing has a good side because my own experience has shown me that good things can come out of bad.

Pinpoint your support: How should I support my focus, based on the topic?
I should give examples from my own personal experience and observations of how something good happened because of something bad.

Try It Yourself

TOPIC B

Some people are cautious in making decisions, while others like to take risks.

Is it better to be a cautious person or a risk taker? Use your personal observations, experience, and knowledge to support your answer.

Read and think: What is the topic asking? (Write the topic as a question in your own words.)

_____

Write a focus statement: What will be my main point? (Answer your question.)

_____

Plan for support: How will I support my focus? (What support does the topic ask for?)

_____

Practice

Read each topic below. Restate the topic as a question, using your own words. Then write a focus statement that answers the question. Finally, write a plan for supporting your focus.

TOPIC C

Many people save "keepsakes," or mementos—small objects that remind them of a person or an experience that was important to them.

Are these kinds of mementos important to you? In your essay, explain why or why not. Use your personal observations, experience, and knowledge.

Read and think: What is the topic asking? (Write the topic as a question in your own words.)

_____

Write a focus statement: What will be my main point? (Answer your question.)

_____

Pinpoint your support: How will I support my focus? (What support does the topic ask for?)

_____

TOPIC D

Pets are important members of many households.

Why are pets important to many people? Use your personal observations, experience, and knowledge to support your answer.

Read and think: What is the topic asking? (Write the topic as a question in your own words.)

_____

Write a focus statement: What will be my main point? (Answer your question.)

_____

Pinpoint your support: How will I support my focus? (What support does the topic ask for?)

_____

Use the checklist on page 40 to review your work.

STEP 3

Plan Before You Write

When you have to write an essay within a time limit, it's easy to fall into the trap of thinking that you should use all your time to write the essay. However, *you will write a higher scoring essay if you take time to plan first.* **Planning** a test essay involves thinking of and listing supporting ideas and details, then grouping related ideas. Each group becomes a paragraph. Planning your essay in this way will help give it a clear **organization** that the essay scorer will be able to see.

E X A M P L E

TOPIC A	Organizational Plan
The saying "Every cloud has a silver lining" means that every bad thing has a good side. In your experience, is this idea true? Use your personal observations, experience, and knowledge to support your answer. **Focus statement:** *My experience has shown me that good things can come out of bad.* **Support:** *examples from my own personal experience and observations of how something good happened because of something bad*	**Paragraph 1 Supporting Idea:** got laid off from my job, but then I got a better one **Details:** very discouraged at first now my work is much more interesting **Paragraph 2 Supporting Idea:** when our apartment went condo, we bought our unit **Details:** thought we had to move, very upset found first-time home buyers program **Paragraph 3 Supporting Idea:** Carly's injury, missed sports season **Details:** spent more time at home understand teen girls much better now!

Try It Yourself

TOPIC B

Some people are cautious in making decisions, while others like to take risks.

Is it better to be a cautious person or a risk taker? Use your personal observations, experience, and knowledge to support your answer.

Review your focus statement and pinpointed support for Topic B (see page 12).

Organizational plan: List supporting idea and details for each supporting paragraph:

Paragraph 1 Supporting Idea: _____

Details: _____

Paragraph 2 Supporting Idea: _____

Details: _____

Paragraph 3 Supporting Idea: _____

Details: _____

Check: Does each paragraph develop one idea? Does each paragraph support the focus?

Practice

Review your work on Topics C and D (see page 13). Write a plan for organizing supporting paragraphs for an essay based on each topic. Your plan should show how your paragraphs will support your focus statement and respond to the overall topic. You may want to start a list on another sheet of paper and then organize your ideas on the lines below.

Review your focus statement and pinpointed support for Topic C (see page 13).

Organizational plan: List a supporting idea and details for each supporting paragraph:

Paragraph 1 Supporting Idea: _____

Details: _____

_____

Paragraph 2 Supporting Idea: _____

Details: _____

_____

Paragraph 3 Supporting Idea: _____

Details: _____

_____

Check: Does each paragraph develop one idea? Does each paragraph support the focus?

Review your focus statement and pinpointed support for Topic D (see page 13).

Organizational plan: List a supporting idea and details for each supporting paragraph:

Paragraph 1 Supporting Idea: _____

Details: _____

_____

Paragraph 2 Supporting Idea: _____

Details: _____

_____

Paragraph 3 Supporting Idea: _____

Details: _____

_____

Check: Does each paragraph develop one idea? Does each paragraph support the focus?

Use the checklist on page 40 to review your work.

STEP 3

Develop Your Support

In addition to organization, GED essay scorers look for **development** of supporting ideas. That means you will need to include **specific details, examples, facts,** or **reasons** to support the main idea of each paragraph as well as the focus statement of your entire essay. Your organizational plan will provide a structure for your essay and a few details to get you started. However, as you are writing, you should try to include even more supporting details. In the example below, see how the writer develops a detailed, interesting paragraph based on his organizational plan.

EXAMPLE

TOPIC A, Paragraph 1 Plan	Developing Support
Paragraph 1 Supporting Idea: got laid off from my job, but then I got a better one **Details:** very discouraged at first now my work is much more interesting	Two years ago, I was laid off from a job in tech support at a big company. Getting laid off was a shock. I thought it was some of the worst luck I ever had. But I was wrong. If I hadn't lost that job, I wouldn't have gone looking for a new one. Now I work in a smaller company where I have to do different kinds of tasks. I don't have the same routine all day long, and I'm never bored, like I was at my old job. The pay is just as good, and best of all, I'm learning new skills all the time.

Try It Yourself

Review your organizational plan for Topic B (see page 14).

Develop your support: Write two detailed paragraphs based on your plan.

Paragraph 1: _____

_____

_____

_____

_____

Paragraph 2: _____

_____

_____

_____

_____

Check: Does each paragraph offer the reader specific details, examples, facts, or reasons? Does it help create a picture of what you're describing?

Practice

Now develop your support for Topics C and D (see page 13). Write detailed paragraphs based on each plan.

Review your organizational plan for Topic C (see page 15).

Develop your support: Write two detailed paragraphs based on your plan.

Paragraph 1: _____

_____

_____

_____

_____

Paragraph 2: _____

_____

_____

_____

_____

Check: Does each paragraph offer the reader specific details, examples, facts, or reasons? Does it help create a picture of what you're describing?

Review your organizational plan for Topic D (see page 15).

Develop your support: Write two detailed paragraphs based on your plan. Write a third detailed paragraph on another sheet of paper.

Paragraph 1: _____

_____

_____

_____

_____

Paragraph 2: _____

_____

_____

_____

_____

Check: Does each paragraph offer the reader specific details, examples, facts, or reasons? Does it help create a picture of what you're describing?

Use the checklist on page 41 to review your work.

Finalize Your Essay to Make a Good Impression

If you were writing a complete GED essay on Topic D right now, you would have a focus statement and three developed, supporting paragraphs already written. There are a few steps left for a finished essay: your introduction, conclusion, and final review.

- **Introduction.** When you take the GED test, write your focus statement on the scratch paper that you'll be given. Then leave a few lines at the top of the essay answer sheet so that you can write your introduction *after* you've written the supporting paragraphs. If you're running short on time, your introduction can be just the focus statement. If you have time, write an additional sentence or two to help show the essay scorers how you're responding to the topic.
- **Conclusion.** Bring your essay to a close by restating your most important or valuable point. Then relate that point back to the original essay topic. Your conclusion can be just one or two sentences—like the introduction.
- **Final review.** Read over your essay. Does it make sense? Is anything left out—perhaps a connecting idea or a clarifying word? Check for the errors you make most often in grammar, sentence structure, spelling, punctuation, and other conventions of English. If you make changes, cross out and add words neatly. It's all right to add a new phrase or sentence and draw an arrow to where it belongs in the essay.

EXAMPLE

Topic A Focus Statement

I believe it's true that every bad thing has a good side because my own experience has shown me that good things can come out of bad.

Topic A Introduction

I believe it's true that every bad thing has a good side because my own experience has shown me that good things can come out of bad. At several times in my life, I have found the silver lining behind the dark cloud.

Supporting Paragraph

When my daughter Carly was injured running track, she missed a season. Instead of going to track meets, she was home. Her friends came over to help her with her PT and watch videos. They did makeovers. After that spring, I knew she and her friends alot better—and I like them all better now too!

Paragraph After Final Review

When my daughter Carly was injured running track, she missed a
season. Instead of ~~going to~~ track meets, she was home. Her friends
            —— spending long Saturdays at
            physical therapy
came over to help her with her ~~PT~~ and watch videos. They did makeovers! , and I served pizza
            her   a lot
After that spring, I knew ~~she~~ and her friends ~~alot~~ better—and I like

them all better now too!

Conclusion

So you just never know what will happen in life. It seems things are just as likely to come out well as turn out badly, so you might as well look for that silver lining!

Practice

I. **Write introductions and conclusions for your essays based on Topics B, C, and D. (To review the topics, see pages 12–13.)**

Introduction: Use your focus statement. Add an additional sentence before or after the focus statement that helps explain how your essay will address the topic.

Conclusion: Restate your most important point. Add an additional sentence that reminds the reader how your essay is related to the topic.

Topic B Introduction: _____

_____

_____

Topic B Conclusion: _____

_____

_____

Topic C Introduction: _____

_____

_____

Topic C Conclusion: _____

_____

_____

Topic D Introduction: _____

_____

_____

Topic D Conclusion: _____

_____

_____

II. **Review all your supporting paragraphs for these practice topics, as well as the introductions and conclusions you just wrote. Check for any phrases or words to add. Correct any errors you see. Practice making changes neatly.**

Use the checklist on page 41 to review your work.

Sharpen Your Test-Taking Skills

On pages 27–37, you will find a full-length practice test that will help you get ready for the real GED Writing Test. Before you take the practice test, take this opportunity to review the format and the four different types of multiple-choice questions you'll see in Part I. As you study these sample questions, choose the best answer for each.

<u>Questions 1 through 4</u> are based on the following article.

Read the **direction line.** Notice how many questions will be based on the passage. Also notice what type of writing it is—in this case, an article.

Attention, Drivers!
See That Motorcycle?

(A)

(1) When a motorcycle and a four-wheeled vehicle are involved in a road accident the driver of the four-wheeler is twice as likely to be at fault. (2) Experts on road safety believed that in many cases drivers simply do not notice motorcycles. (3) In fact, experienced motorcycle riders know this one thing, and that thing is that their best defensive driving strategy is to assume they are invisible.

Each passage has **lettered paragraphs and numbered sentences.** These letters and numbers are used in the questions so that you can find the place in the passage each question is based on.

(B)

(4) For example, when an experienced motorcyclist sees a car turning left from the oncoming lane, he or she slows down and stays out of the way of the turning car.

Read the entire passage first, before going on to the questions. You may notice errors in sentences as you read. Keep them in mind. This will give you a head start on answering the questions about those sentences.

(C)

(5) Some motorcyclists deliberately draw attention to themselves. (6) Riders may rev their engines, swing back and forth inside their driving lane, or speed up or slow down just to attract attention. (7) Wearing bright-colored clothing and riding gear is also recommended.

1. Sentence 1: **When a motorcycle and a four-wheeled vehicle are involved in a road accident the driver of the four-wheeler is twice as likely to be at fault.**

   Which correction should be made to sentence 1?

   (1) replace <u>When</u> with <u>Although</u>
   (2) change <u>are</u> to <u>were</u>
   (3) change <u>road</u> to <u>rode</u>
   (4) insert a comma after <u>accident</u>
   (5) no correction is necessary

This question asks "which correction" is needed. It's in the **correction** format, which you can review on pages 4–5. Remember that each answer choice is testing a different possible error. There can only be one error in each sentence.

Try to find the error as you read the sentence, and look for the answer choice that corrects it.

If you can't find an error, try each answer choice in the sentence. You might also see the choice "no correction is necessary." This choice will sometimes be the right one.

2. Sentence 2: **Experts on road safety <u>believed</u> that in many cases drivers simply do not notice motorcycles.**

   Which is the best way to write the underlined portion of this sentence? If the original is the best way, choose option (1).

   (1) believed
   (2) have believed
   (3) believe
   (4) believing
   (5) will believe

3. Sentence 3: **In fact, experienced motorcycle riders know this one thing, and that thing is that their best defensive driving strategy is to assume they are invisible.**

   The most effective revision of sentence 3 would include which group of words?

   (1) know that their
   (2) this one, their best
   (3) know defensive driving
   (4) know this thing that
   (5) know that, however, their

4. Which revision would improve the effectiveness of the article?

   (1) start a new paragraph with sentence 2
   (2) join paragraphs A and B
   (3) remove paragraph B
   (4) join paragraphs B and C
   (5) no revision is necessary

Check answers and explanations on page 41.

This question asks you to consider how to rewrite the underlined part of the sentence. It's in the **revision** format, which you can review on pages 6–7.

Be sure to take into account the entire sentence before you make your choice. Option (1) will always give you the choice of leaving the sentence as is. This choice will sometimes be correct.

This question is in the **construction shift** format, which you can review on pages 8–9. You will not be able to spot an error in the sentence. However, you might notice that it is awkward or repetitive.

First try rearranging the awkward part or eliminating unnecessary words in your head. Then look for the answer choice that fits your revision. If you can't "shift" the sentence on your own, test each answer choice and try to "hear" the rewritten sentence using the words in the choice. Construction shift questions may ask you to rewrite a single sentence, like this one, or combine two sentences into one.

Organization questions, like this one, ask you to make improvements to the passage as a whole or to a particular paragraph. You can review these questions on pages 10–11.

You may have noticed problems with organization as you read the passage. That will help you spot the answer quickly. If you did not, try each answer choice to see if it improves the organization.

STEP 4

Test-Taking Style Self-Evaluation

Thinking about **correction questions,** I feel that
☐ I understand them   ☐ I need more work

Thinking about **revision questions,** I feel that
☐ I understand them   ☐ I need more work

Thinking about **construction shift questions,** I feel that
☐ I understand them   ☐ I need more work

Thinking about **organization questions,** I feel that
☐ I understand them   ☐ I need more work

Practice Test Warm-Up Exercise, Part I

Circle the number of your answer to each practice question. Explain why you chose it. Then read the following page to check your answers and read answer explanations.

<u>Questions 1 through 4</u> refer to the following business letter.

Dear Ms. Maguire:

(A)
(1) I am writing to thank you for your efforts to return my son's Franklin doll, which he left behind in a room in your hotel last week. (2) This doll being my son's favorite companion, we are all delighted to have Franklin back home where he belongs!

(B)
(3) I realize that hotel Managers are very busy. (4) I want you to know how much I appreciate the time you took to find the doll and ship it back to us. (5) You impressed my family and I very much with your kindness. (6) It's too bad that the hotel pool was closed during our visit.

Sincerely,
Tillman Desmet

1. Sentence 2: **This doll being my son's favorite companion, we are all delighted to have Franklin back home where he belongs!**

   The most effective revision of sentence 2 would begin with which group of words?

   (1) Because this doll, being
   (2) We being delighted
   (3) This doll delights
   (4) Because this doll is my
   (5) Having this doll be

   Explanation _____
   _____

2. Sentence 3: **I realize that hotel Managers are very busy.**

   Which correction should be made to sentence 3?

   (1) change <u>I realize</u> to <u>Realizing</u>
   (2) change <u>Managers</u> to <u>managers</u>
   (3) insert a comma after <u>Managers</u>
   (4) change <u>are</u> to <u>is</u>
   (5) no correction is necessary

   Explanation _____
   _____

3. Sentence 5: **You impressed <u>my family and I</u> very much with your kindness.**

   Which is the best way to write the underlined portion? If the original is the best way, choose option (1).

   (1) my family and I
   (2) them and I
   (3) my family and me
   (4) they and I
   (5) we

   Explanation _____
   _____

4. Which revision should be made to the placement of sentence 6?

   (1) move sentence 6 to follow sentence 2
   (2) move sentence 6 to the beginning of paragraph B
   (3) move sentence 6 to follow sentence 3
   (4) remove sentence 6
   (5) no revision is necessary

   Explanation _____
   _____

Warm-Up Part I Answers and Explanations

Check your answer and read the explanations. Then evaluate how you did.

1. **(4)   Because this doll is my**

   Explanation: This **construction shift** question requires you to figure out a complete sentence that would improve sentence 2 and include one of the answer choices. The complete sentence would be, *Because this doll is my son's favorite companion, we are all delighted to have Franklin back home where he belongs!*

   The other choices are incorrect because none of them leads to an effective, smooth sentence that keeps the meaning of the original.

2. **(2)   change <u>Managers</u> to <u>managers</u>**

   Explanation: To answer this **correction** question, you need to realize that the word *managers* should not be capitalized because it is not a proper noun.

   Choice (1) is incorrect because it would remove the subject from the sentence, creating a fragment.

   Choice (3) is incorrect because a comma here would be unnecessary.

   Choice (4) is incorrect because it would create an error in subject-verb agreement.

   Choice (5) is incorrect because a correction is needed.

3. **(3)   my family and me**

   Explanation: To answer this **revision** question, you need to realize that the pronoun is the object of the verb *impressed*, so it should be the objective pronoun *me*, not the subjective pronoun *I*.

   Choice (1) is incorrect because it is the same as the original sentence, which is wrong.

   Choice (2) is incorrect because it uses the objective pronoun *them* but the subjective pronoun *I*. Also, the word that *them* refers to is not clear.

   Choice (4) is incorrect because it uses two subjective pronouns when objective pronouns are needed.

   Choice (5) is incorrect because it uses the subjective pronoun *we* instead of an objective pronoun.

4. **(4)   remove sentence 6**

   Explanation: To answer this **organization** question, you need to realize that sentence 6 is not related to the topic of the letter. Therefore, it should be removed.

   All the other choices are incorrect because they involve simply moving sentence 6 or leaving it where it is.

Warm-Up Part I Self-Evaluation

Question 1 ☐ Correct   ☐ Incorrect   **Question 3** ☐ Correct   ☐ Incorrect
Question 2 ☐ Correct   ☐ Incorrect   **Question 4** ☐ Correct   ☐ Incorrect

When I take the Practice GED Writing Test, Part I, I need to pay special attention to

_____

_____

_____

_____

Practice Test Warm-Up Exercise, Part II

Write a practice essay based on Topic E, according to the steps listed below. Use a clock or timer to help you complete the steps in the time suggested. You will need scratch paper as well as lined paper for writing your essay.

Begin working on your essay as soon as you have read the topic. Keep track of the time as you work. Stop after 45 minutes.

TOPIC E

Some people say that they have a hard time applying what they learned in school to real-life tasks and challenges.

Do you agree with this view? In your essay, explain why or why not. Use your personal observations, experience, and knowledge to support your answer.

Step 1: Respond to the Topic
(1–2 minutes)

1. Write the topic as a question in your own words.

2. Answer the question with a focus statement that will be the main point of your essay.

3. Pinpoint how you will support the focus.

Step 2: Plan Before You Write
(5–8 minutes)

1. Jot down one supporting idea and list a few details that you will write about in each supporting paragraph of your essay. Try for three supporting ideas and paragraphs.

2. Check to make sure each paragraph will support the focus.

Step 3: Develop Your Ideas As You Write
(20–25 minutes)

1. Leave several blank lines at the top of your paper so that you can write your introduction last.

2. Write the supporting paragraphs of your essay. Be sure to use your organizational plan.

3. As you write each paragraph, add specific details, examples, facts, and reasons.

Step 4: Finalize Your Essay
(10–15 minutes)

1. Write the introduction to your essay. Use your focus statement and show how it relates to the essay topic.

2. Write the conclusion. Restate the most important point and relate it to the essay topic.

3. Review your essay as a whole. Make any corrections, deletions, or insertions neatly. (Do not make a new copy of your essay.)

Use the Practice Essay Review Guide on the following page to review your essay.

Practice Essay Review Guide

You can use this guide to review any practice essay for the GED Writing Test. This guide is based on the official GED Essay Scoring Guide (see page 44).

Don't review your essay right after you have written it. Set it aside for a day if possible, or at least for a few hours. When you are ready to review the essay, read it carefully, then answer the following questions.

Response to the Prompt	Yes	Somewhat	No
Does the essay address the topic given? Does the essay have a focus? Is the focus maintained throughout the essay?			
Organization			
Does the essay have paragraphs that organize ideas and details? Does each paragraph develop a different supporting idea? Is there an introduction and conclusion?			
Development and Details			
Are there details that clearly relate to the focus and the topic? Are there specific details that illustrate the essay's points?			
Conventions of Edited English			
Does the essay use sentence structure effectively to convey ideas? Are the grammar and mechanics (spelling, capitalization, punctuation) generally correct in the essay?			
Word Choice			
Are the words appropriate for formal essay writing? Are the words interesting and precise?			

Warm-Up Part II Self-Evaluation

Use the checklist below to identify your strengths and weaknesses in essay writing.

Response to the Prompt: ☐ Strong ☐ Weak
Organization: ☐ Strong ☐ Weak
Development and Details: ☐ Strong ☐ Weak
Conventions of Edited English: ☐ Strong ☐ Weak
Word Choice: ☐ Strong ☐ Weak

I can manage my time well in a 45-minute practice essay: ☐ Yes ☐ No

When I take the Practice GED Writing Test, Part II, I need to pay special attention to

_____

_____

Strategies for Passing
the GED Language Arts, Writing Test

Strategies for Part I

- **Read each passage carefully before you begin answering the questions based on it**. Get a head start on the questions by watching out for errors or other problems. Even if it takes you a few minutes to read each passage, it's a wise way to spend the time.

- **Pay special attention to verbs and pronouns in the passages.** Some questions will ask you to correct errors that are based on the passage as a whole. For example, you may not realize that a verb in the past tense is incorrect if you are looking at just that sentence. But if the rest of the passage is in the present tense, the past tense verb may be wrong.

- **Pay attention to the format of each question.** In this book, you have reviewed four basic types of questions: correction, revision, construction shift, and organization. Construction shift and organization also have several variations, as you have probably noticed. This means that you should read each question carefully to be sure you understand what it's asking you to do.

- **Remember that not all questions contain errors.** Some questions will ask you to *improve* a sentence rather than to correct an error. If the writing is awkward or repetitive, look for an answer choice that smoothes out the problem. If you are sure that a sentence is correct and well written, look for an answer choice that allows you to leave it alone. In revision questions, choice (1) is always the same as the original sentence. In correction questions, choice (5) may be *no correction is necessary*. Organization questions may also have choice (5) *no revision is necessary*. Look carefully at <u>all</u> the answer choices before you jump to conclusions. Be sure to think about the effectiveness of the writing as a whole.

- **Work steadily.** The more time you spend struggling with any one question, the less time you'll have to finish. If you're not sure of an answer, eliminate choices that are clearly wrong, take your best guess, and move on. Make a light pencil mark next to questions that you'd like to return to if there is time at the end of the test.

- **Answer every question.** *Always* mark an answer for each question, even if you are guessing. This will keep you from losing your place on the answer sheet. If you guess right, you'll get credit for the answer! If you guess wrong, you will not get credit, but you will not lose points as you would on some tests.

You can go on to Part II, the essay, as soon as you finish the multiple-choice questions on Part I. The test administrator will tell you when 45 minutes are left; then you must begin Part II even if you haven't finished Part I. If you finish your essay before the 45 minutes are over, you may return to Part I if you have unfinished questions or to check the multiple-choice portion of the test.

Strategies for Part II

- **Plan your essay first.** To get a high score, you must establish a focus for your essay that clearly addresses the prompt and then stick to your focus. That can come only with a plan.

- **Manage your time.** Spend up to 10 minutes on your focus and organizational plan, 20 to 25 minutes writing and developing, and 10 to 15 minutes reviewing and finalizing.

- **Use details and examples to support your ideas.** Use your life experience! Use what you've seen, what you know, and what you've experienced to illustrate the points in your essay.

- **Edit neatly.** Do not write a draft copy of your essay and then copy it over on the answer sheet—this takes too much time. The essay readers do not expect a perfect copy. It's fine to make changes and corrections to your essay. Just use neat, clear marks.

Practice GED Language Arts, Writing Test

Directions

This **_Practice GED Language Arts, Writing Test_** is similar to what you will see on the actual GED. This test includes both multiple-choice questions in Part I and an essay in Part II. These directions apply to Part I; a separate set of directions is given for the essay.

The multiple-choice section consists of passages with lettered paragraphs and numbered sentences. Some of the sentences contain errors in sentence structure, usage, punctuation, capitalization, or spelling. After reading the numbered sentences, answer the multiple-choice questions that follow. Some questions refer to sentences that are correct as written. The best answer to these questions is the one that leaves the sentence as originally written. The best answer for some questions is the one that produces a sentence that is consistent with the verb tense and point of view used throughout the text.

You will have 120 minutes to complete this test. You will spend 75 minutes on Part I, leaving 45 minutes for the essay. Work carefully, but do not spend too much time on any one question. Be sure to answer every question. You may copy and use the answer sheet below, or you may write your answers on another sheet of paper.

After you have finished Part I, write the essay and then check your work against the answers and explanations on pages 41–43. Use the GED Personal Coach™ on pages 38–39 to help you make your final plan.

You may begin now.

STEP 4

1. ① ② ③ ④ ⑤   11. ① ② ③ ④ ⑤   21. ① ② ③ ④ ⑤   31. ① ② ③ ④ ⑤   41. ① ② ③ ④ ⑤

2. ① ② ③ ④ ⑤   12. ① ② ③ ④ ⑤   22. ① ② ③ ④ ⑤   32. ① ② ③ ④ ⑤   42. ① ② ③ ④ ⑤

3. ① ② ③ ④ ⑤   13. ① ② ③ ④ ⑤   23. ① ② ③ ④ ⑤   33. ① ② ③ ④ ⑤   43. ① ② ③ ④ ⑤

4. ① ② ③ ④ ⑤   14. ① ② ③ ④ ⑤   24. ① ② ③ ④ ⑤   34. ① ② ③ ④ ⑤   44. ① ② ③ ④ ⑤

5. ① ② ③ ④ ⑤   15. ① ② ③ ④ ⑤   25. ① ② ③ ④ ⑤   35. ① ② ③ ④ ⑤   45. ① ② ③ ④ ⑤

6. ① ② ③ ④ ⑤   16. ① ② ③ ④ ⑤   26. ① ② ③ ④ ⑤   36. ① ② ③ ④ ⑤   46. ① ② ③ ④ ⑤

7. ① ② ③ ④ ⑤   17. ① ② ③ ④ ⑤   27. ① ② ③ ④ ⑤   37. ① ② ③ ④ ⑤   47. ① ② ③ ④ ⑤

8. ① ② ③ ④ ⑤   18. ① ② ③ ④ ⑤   28. ① ② ③ ④ ⑤   38. ① ② ③ ④ ⑤   48. ① ② ③ ④ ⑤

9. ① ② ③ ④ ⑤   19. ① ② ③ ④ ⑤   29. ① ② ③ ④ ⑤   39. ① ② ③ ④ ⑤   49. ① ② ③ ④ ⑤

10. ① ② ③ ④ ⑤   20. ① ② ③ ④ ⑤   30. ① ② ③ ④ ⑤   40. ① ② ③ ④ ⑤   50. ① ② ③ ④ ⑤

Part I

Directions: Choose the <u>one best answer</u> to each question.

<u>Questions 1 through 5</u> are based on the following article.

New Task Force on Transit

(A)

(1) Commuters in the Kenton area currently have few options for getting to work, other than driving there own cars. (2) Cars can be expensive to own and operate. (3) Bus routes established in the 1960s fan out from the old city center but they do not reflect more recent patterns of development.

(B)

(4) Now a task force has been established. (5) This task force will assess commuters' needs across the region. (6) The task force has been asked to think about a range of options, including expanded bus service, company-sponsored vans, carpools, and even to consider light rail development.

1. Sentence 1: **Commuters in the Kenton area currently have few options for getting to work, other than driving there own cars.**

   Which correction should be made to sentence 1?

   (1) change <u>area</u> to <u>Area</u>
   (2) insert a comma after <u>area</u>
   (3) change <u>have</u> to <u>having</u>
   (4) replace <u>there</u> with <u>they're</u>
   (5) replace <u>there</u> with <u>their</u>

2. Which revision should be made to the placement of sentence 2?

   (1) remove sentence 2
   (2) move sentence 2 to the beginning of paragraph A
   (3) move sentence 2 to follow sentence 3
   (4) move sentence 2 to the beginning of paragraph B
   (5) no revision is necessary

3. Sentence 3: **Bus routes established in the 1960s fan out from the old city <u>center but</u> they do not reflect more recent patterns of development.**

   Which is the best way to write the underlined portion of this sentence? If the original is the best way, choose option (1).

   (1) center but
   (2) center, but
   (3) center. But
   (4) center however
   (5) center and

4. Sentences 4 and 5: **Now a task force has been established. This task force will assess commuters' needs across the region.**

   The most effective combination of sentences 4 and 5 would include which group of words?

   (1) Now that a task force has been
   (2) Establishing a task force
   (3) established, and it will be assessing
   (4) A task force having been established
   (5) has been established to assess

5. Sentence 6: **The task force has been asked to think about a range of options, including expanded bus service, company-sponsored vans, carpools, and even to consider light rail development.**

   Which correction should be made to sentence 6?

   (1) remove the comma after <u>service</u>
   (2) remove the comma after <u>vans</u>
   (3) insert a comma after <u>even</u>
   (4) remove <u>to consider</u>
   (5) no correction is necessary

Questions 6 through 10 are based on the following passage.

Public Speaking—Without Fear!

(A)
(1) If your number one fear is public speaking, you're not alone. (2) Many Americans agree with you. (3) However, the good news is that most people, meaning those people who stand up in front of groups and talk, are scared. (4) The *biggest* difference between the audience and the speaker is that the speaker is the person in the front of the room!

(B)
(5) First you need an attention grabber or strong opening, for your speech. (6) You don't have to tell a joke. (7) One might begin with a question, a startling fact, or a story. (8) Then be giving your listeners a straightforward message in a direct style. (9) End by thanking the people in your audience for their attention, and encourage them to talk with you individually after the program.

6. Sentence 3: **However, the good news is that most people, meaning those people who stand up in front of groups and talk, are scared.**

   The most effective revision of sentence 3 would include which group of words?

   (1) most people are scared
   (2) people, meaning to stand up and talk
   (3) most people who stand up
   (4) the good news is that standing up
   (5) Scaring the people who stand up

7. Which sentence would be most effective if inserted at the beginning of paragraph B?

   (1) It's easy to scare someone giving a talk.
   (2) A good speech must have a beginning, a middle, and an end.
   (3) You should open any speech in a strong way to show your authority.
   (4) The speaker is just the person in the front of the room, and that can be you.
   (5) Giving a speech is not as difficult as you think, as long as you practice first.

8. Sentence 5: **First you need an attention grabber or strong opening, for your speech.**

   Which correction should be made to sentence 5?

   (1) replace you need with needing
   (2) change need to needed
   (3) insert a comma after grabber
   (4) replace for with four
   (5) replace your with you're

9. Sentence 7: **One might begin with a question, a startling fact, or a story.**

   Which correction should be made to sentence 7?

   (1) replace One with You
   (2) change might begin to began
   (3) insert a comma after begin
   (4) remove the comma after question
   (5) no correction is necessary

10. Sentence 8: **Then be giving your listeners a straightforward message in a direct style.**

    Which is the best way to write the underlined portion of this sentence? If the original is the best way, choose option (1).

    (1) be giving
    (2) giving
    (3) should give
    (4) have given
    (5) give

Questions 11 through 23 are based on the following business document.

(A)

(1) Tom's Cleaning Service offers window washing for residential and commercial properties. (2) Our competitive rates based on the number, size, and types of windows. (3) To see our rates for various windows please refer to the enclosed rate sheet. (4) We are prompt and thorough, and we are courteous!

(B)

(5) Please call if you would like me to visit your home or business, for the purpose of determining a price. (6) If you and me go over your requirements in detail, I will guarantee your price in advance.

(C)

(7) We agree on a date for your job and schedule a crew. (8) Depending on the weather, they may have to adjust the timing for outside work. (9) One does not allow crews to work on sloping roofs in wet weather. (10) At Tom's, we know that windows are fragile and costly. (11) Keeping the protection of your windows in mind, our workers are carefully trained. (12) We are also fully insured.

(D)

(13) Clean windows let in more light and improve you're view. (14) Let us bring you, the clear appeal of clean windows!

11. Sentence 2: **Our competitive rates <u>based</u> on the number, size, and types of windows.**

    Which is the best way to write the underlined portion of this sentence? If the original is the best way, choose option (1).

    (1) based
    (2) been based
    (3) basing
    (4) is based
    (5) are based

12. Sentence 3: **To see our rates for various windows please refer to the enclosed rate sheet.**

    Which correction should be made to sentence 3?

    (1) replace <u>our</u> with <u>hour</u>
    (2) insert a comma after <u>rates</u>
    (3) insert a comma after <u>windows</u>
    (4) insert a comma after <u>please</u>
    (5) no correction is necessary

13. Sentence 4: **We are <u>prompt and thorough, and we are</u> courteous!**

    Which is the best way to write the underlined portion of this sentence? If the original is the best way, choose option (1).

    (1) prompt and thorough, and we are
    (2) being prompt, thorough, and are
    (3) prompt, thorough, and
    (4) prompt and thorough, also
    (5) prompt, thorough, and are

14. Sentence 5: **Please call if you would like me to visit your home or business, for the purpose of determining a price.**

    The most effective revision of sentence 5 would include which group of words?

    (1) your home or business to determine
    (2) Determining a price for your home
    (3) home or business, determining a price
    (4) visiting your home or business for
    (5) to determine a price at your home or

15. Sentence 6: **If you and me go over your requirements in detail, I will guarantee your price in advance.**

    Which correction should be made to sentence 6?

    (1) replace <u>If</u> with <u>Since</u>
    (2) change <u>me</u> to <u>I</u>
    (3) change <u>go</u> to <u>went</u>
    (4) remove the comma after <u>detail</u>
    (5) change <u>will guarantee</u> to <u>guaranteed</u>

16. Sentence 7: **We agree on a date for your job and schedule a crew.**

    Which correction should be made to sentence 7?

    (1) replace <u>We</u> with <u>You and me</u>
    (2) change <u>agree</u> to <u>will agree</u>
    (3) insert a comma after <u>job</u>
    (4) change <u>schedule</u> to <u>scheduling</u>
    (5) no correction is necessary

17. Sentence 8: **Depending on the weather, <u>they</u> may have to adjust the timing for outside work.**

    Which is the best way to write the underlined portion of this sentence? If the original is the best way, choose option (1).

    (1) they
    (2) you
    (3) one
    (4) us
    (5) the crew

18. Sentence 9: **<u>One does</u> not allow crews to work on sloping roofs in wet weather.**

    Which is the best way to write the underlined portion of this sentence? If the original is the best way, choose option (1).

    (1) One does
    (2) You do
    (3) They do
    (4) We do
    (5) It does

19. Which revision would improve the effectiveness of the letter?

    (1) begin a new paragraph with sentence 3
    (2) combine paragraphs A and B
    (3) begin a new paragraph with sentence 10
    (4) combine paragraphs C and D
    (5) remove paragraph D

20. Sentence 11: **Keeping the protection of your windows in mind, <u>our workers are carefully trained.</u>**

    Which is the best way to write the underlined portion of this sentence? If the original is the best way, choose option (1).

    (1) our workers are carefully trained
    (2) we have carefully trained our workers
    (3) your workers will be carefully trained
    (4) training our workers is careful
    (5) our worker training is careful

21. Which revision should be made to the placement of sentence 12?

    (1) remove sentence 12
    (2) move sentence 12 to follow sentence 4
    (3) move sentence 12 to follow sentence 9
    (4) move sentence 12 to follow sentence 13
    (5) no revision is necessary

22. Sentence 13: **Clean windows let in more light and improve you're view.**

    Which correction should be made to sentence 13?

    (1) insert a comma after <u>windows</u>
    (2) insert a comma after <u>light</u>
    (3) change <u>improve</u> to <u>improving</u>
    (4) replace <u>you're</u> with <u>your</u>
    (5) no correction is necessary

23. Sentence 14: **Let us bring you, the clear appeal of clean windows!**

    Which correction should be made to sentence 14?

    (1) replace <u>us</u> with <u>them</u>
    (2) change <u>bring</u> to <u>be bringing</u>
    (3) remove the comma after <u>you</u>
    (4) insert a comma after <u>appeal</u>
    (5) no correction is necessary

Questions 24 through 29 are based on the following announcement.

Rose Park Facility Improvement

(A)

(1) The public is invited to comment on plans to improve Rose park at an open meeting on April 27. (2) Construction of these improvements is scheduled to begin by September of this year. (3) The meeting will begin at 7 P.M. with a presentation on the design plans by the contractor, City Play, Inc. (4) City Play designers and the park board hear statements from the public beginning at 8 P.M (5) There also will be an open discussion and question period.

(B)

(6) The overall plan for park improvements include play equipment, landscaping, and a community garden. (7) Also under consideration is several small pavilions for group gatherings. (8) To learn more about the project schedule and plans, call the office of the park board or visit our Web site.

24. Sentence 1: **The public is invited to comment on plans to improve Rose park at an open meeting on April 27.**

    Which correction should be made to sentence 1?

    (1) change <u>is</u> to <u>being</u>
    (2) insert a comma after <u>invited</u>
    (3) insert a comma after <u>plans</u>
    (4) change <u>park</u> to <u>Park</u>
    (5) change <u>April</u> to <u>april</u>

25. Which revision should be made to the placement of sentence 2?

    (1) remove sentence 2
    (2) move sentence 2 to follow sentence 3
    (3) move sentence 2 to follow sentence 5
    (4) move sentence to the beginning of paragraph B
    (5) move sentence 2 to follow sentence 7

26. Sentence 3: **The meeting will begin at 7 P.M. with a presentation on the design plans by the contractor, City Play, Inc.**

    Which correction should be made to sentence 3?

    (1) replace <u>will begin</u> with <u>beginning</u>
    (2) insert a comma after <u>begin</u>
    (3) change <u>contractor</u> to <u>Contractor</u>
    (4) remove the comma after <u>contractor</u>
    (5) no correction is necessary

27. Sentence 4: **City Play designers and the park board <u>hear</u> statements from the public beginning at 8 P.M.**

    Which is the best way to write the underlined portion of this sentence? If the original is the best way, choose option (1).

    (1) hear
    (2) hearing
    (3) heard
    (4) will hear
    (5) hears

28. Sentence 6: **The overall plan for park improvements <u>include</u> play equipment, landscaping, and a community garden.**

    Which is the best way to write the underlined portion of this sentence? If the original is the best way, choose option (1).

    (1) include
    (2) included
    (3) includes
    (4) including
    (5) had included

29. Sentence 7: **Also under consideration <u>is</u> several small pavilions for group gatherings.**

    Which is the best way to write the underlined portion of this sentence? If the original is the best way, choose option (1).

    (1) is
    (2) are
    (3) been
    (4) were
    (5) was

Questions 30 through 33 are based on the following article.

How Yeast Works

(A)

(1) For centuries people have used yeast. (2) Yeast is a vital ingredient in many types of breads and baked goods. (3) This is because it is the ingredient that makes the dough fluff up and rise. (4) How does yeast work?

(B)

(5) When dough is made with yeast and left to rise, the yeast cells eat sugars in the dough. (6) The cells are eating these sugars and taking in oxygen, and at the same time they divide and produce new yeast cells.

(C)

(7) What makes the dough actually rise, however, is that the yeast cells are also giving off carbon dioxide gas. (8) The gas causes the dough to expand.

(D)

(9) The yeast's food supply of sugar diminishes, the rising process slows down. (10) Eventually, the rising stops.

30. Sentences 2 and 3: **Yeast is a vital ingredient in many types of breads and baked goods. This is because it is the ingredient that makes the dough fluff up and rise.**

    Which is the best way to write the underlined portion of these sentences? If the original is the best way, choose option (1).

    (1) goods. This is because it is the ingredient that
    (2) goods, this because it
    (3) goods, this is because it is the ingredient that
    (4) goods and because it
    (5) goods because it

31. Sentence 6: **The cells are eating these sugars and taking in oxygen, and at the same time they divide and produce new yeast cells.**

    If you rewrote sentence 6 beginning with

    As the cells eat these sugars and take in oxygen,

    the next word should be

    (1) they
    (2) when
    (3) if
    (4) and
    (5) then

32. Sentence 9: **The yeast's food supply of sugar diminishes, the rising process slows down.**

    Which is the best way to write the underlined portion of this sentence? If the original is the best way, choose option (1).

    (1) The yeast's food supply of sugar diminishes,
    (2) As the yeast's food supply of sugar diminishes,
    (3) Before the yeast's food supply of sugar diminishes,
    (4) Given that the yeast's food supply of sugar is diminishing,
    (5) Diminishing the yeast's food supply of sugar,

33. Which revision would improve the effectiveness of the article?

    (1) combine paragraphs A and B
    (2) remove paragraph B
    (3) combine paragraphs C and D
    (4) remove paragraph D
    (5) no revision is necessary

STEP 4

Questions 34 through 45 are based on the following article.

How to Conduct Effective Meetings

(A)
(1) Do you dread meetings refuse to run them, and complain about them afterward? (2) We can all make this situation better by using a few essential strategies for making meetings effective.

(B)
(3) The first principal for an effective meeting is that you must not waste people's time. (4) You should call a meeting only if you have to, like when there is no other way to get the work done. (5) Plan the agenda in advance. (6) Include the ending time of the meeting. (7) Distribute them and a list of any materials people need to bring. (8) During the meeting, keep the discussion focused on the agenda other issues should be dealt with later.

(C)
(9) The second strategy for an effective meeting was to make it a comfortable experience. (10) Refreshments, even something as simple as some sodas and a bucket of ice, make people feel appreciated. (11) A fake meeting is a good way to pull off a surprise party or shower. (12) If the meeting will be longer than one hour, scheduling a short break so people can use the restroom. (13) Make sure that the room is comfortably cool if it's Summer. (14) If possible, meet in the morning when people still feeling fresh.

(D)
(15) Finally, be sure to follow up. (16) As part of the meeting assign steps that individuals should take next. (17) Make a note of all the participants' follow-up responsibilities, and don't forget their deadlines too. (18) Finally, thank people for their contributions!

34. Sentence 1: **Do you dread meetings refuse to run them, and complain about them afterward?**

Which correction should be made to sentence 1?

(1) replace <u>Do</u> with <u>Does</u>
(2) insert a comma after <u>meetings</u>
(3) change <u>refuse</u> to <u>refusing</u>
(4) remove the comma after <u>them</u>
(5) change <u>complain</u> to <u>complaining</u>

35. Sentence 3: **The first principal for an effective meeting is that you must not waste people's time.**

Which correction should be made to sentence 3?

(1) replace <u>principal</u> with <u>principle</u>
(2) insert a comma after <u>meeting</u>
(3) change <u>is</u> to <u>was</u>
(4) change <u>waste</u> to <u>have wasted</u>
(5) no correction is necessary

36. Sentence 4: **You should call a meeting only if you have to, like when there is no other way to get the work done.**

The most effective revision of sentence 4 would include which group of words?

(1) have to, there being no other way to
(2) You should not call a meeting
(3) If no other way to get the work done,
(4) Call a meeting only if there is
(5) If a meeting is the only way to

37. Sentence 7: **Distribute them and a list of any materials people need to bring.**

Which correction should be made to sentence 7?

(1) change <u>Distribute</u> to <u>Distributing</u>
(2) replace <u>them</u> with <u>the agenda</u>
(3) insert a comma after <u>them</u>
(4) insert a comma after <u>materials</u>
(5) change <u>need</u> to <u>needs</u>

38. Sentence 8: **During the meeting, keep the discussion focused on the <u>agenda other</u> issues should be dealt with later.**

Which is the best way to write the underlined portion of this sentence? If the original is the best way, choose option (1).

(1) agenda other
(2) agenda, other
(3) agenda. Other
(4) agenda, with other
(5) agenda and other

39. Sentence 9: **The second strategy for an effective meeting <u>was</u> to make it a comfortable experience.**

Which is the best way to write the underlined portion of this sentence? If the original is the best way, choose option (1).

(1) was
(2) were
(3) be
(4) are
(5) is

40. Which revision would improve the effectiveness of paragraph C?

(1) remove sentence 10
(2) move sentence 11 to follow sentence 9
(3) move sentence 11 to follow sentence 14
(4) remove sentence 11
(5) no revision is necessary

41. Sentence 12: **If the meeting will be longer than one hour, <u>scheduling</u> a short break so people can use the restroom.**

Which is the best way to write the underlined portion of this sentence? If the original is the best way, choose option (1).

(1) scheduling
(2) scheduled
(3) have scheduled
(4) will be scheduled
(5) schedule

42. Sentence 13: **Make sure that the room is comfortably cool if it's Summer.**

Which correction should be made to sentence 13?

(1) change <u>Make</u> to <u>Making</u>
(2) insert a comma after <u>sure</u>
(3) insert a comma after <u>cool</u>
(4) replace <u>it's</u> with <u>its</u>
(5) change <u>Summer</u> to <u>summer</u>

43. Sentence 14: **If possible, meet in the morning when people still <u>feeling</u> fresh.**

Which is the best way to write the underlined portion of this sentence? If the original is the best way, choose option (1).

(1) feeling
(2) have felt
(3) felt
(4) feel
(5) were feeling

44. Sentence 16: **As part of the meeting assign steps that individuals should take next.**

Which correction should be made to sentence 16?

(1) insert a comma after <u>meeting</u>
(2) change <u>assign</u> to <u>be assigning</u>
(3) insert a comma after <u>steps</u>
(4) change <u>take</u> to <u>have taken</u>
(5) no correction is necessary

45. Sentence 17: **Make a note of all the participants' follow-up responsibilities, and don't forget their deadlines too.**

The most effective revision of sentence 17 would include which group of words?

(1) Make, but don't forget
(2) responsibilities and their deadlines
(3) Without forgetting their deadlines,
(4) Noting that the meeting
(5) following up with responsibilities and

Questions 46 through 50 are based on the following report.

Traffic Department Report: Need for New Traffic Signal

(1) There's a need for a new traffic signal. (2) Our review of accidents at the intersection of Lake Street and Highway 2 has brung a clear pattern to our attention. (3) Drivers did not see the stop sign in the eastbound lane of Lake Street in time because it was not visible around the curve just before the intersection. (4) A signal light, which is more visible from a longer distance, helps solve this problem. (5) There has been three previous reviews of traffic accidents at this corner, and a signal light was recommended each time.

46. Which is the most effective rewrite of sentence 1?

(1) Traffic accidents are a problem in the community.
(2) More traffic signal lights are needed.
(3) The Traffic Department is recommending an additional traffic signal.
(4) Traffic signals are beneficial to drivers.
(5) Some people think we have enough traffic signals, but we disagree.

47. Sentence 2: **Our review of accidents at the intersection of Lake Street and Highway 2 has brung a clear pattern to our attention.**

Which correction should be made to sentence 2?

(1) change <u>Street</u> to <u>street</u>
(2) change <u>Highway</u> to <u>highway</u>
(3) insert a comma after <u>2</u>
(4) change <u>brung</u> to <u>brought</u>
(5) no correction is necessary

48. Sentence 3: **Drivers did not see the stop sign in the eastbound lane of Lake Street in <u>time because it</u> was not visible around the curve just before the intersection.**

Which is the best way to write the underlined portion of this sentence? If the original is the best way, choose option (1).

(1) time because it
(2) time, and it
(3) time. This
(4) time although it
(5) time it

49. Sentence 4: **A signal light, which is more visible from a longer distance, <u>helps</u> solve this problem.**

Which is the best way to write the underlined portion of this sentence? If the original is the best way, choose option (1).

(1) helps
(2) helping
(3) would help
(4) helped
(5) help

50. Sentence 5: **There has been three previous reviews of traffic accidents at this corner, and a signal light was recommended each time.**

Which correction should be made to sentence 5?

(1) change <u>has</u> to <u>have</u>
(2) change <u>has been</u> to <u>being</u>
(3) remove the comma after <u>corner</u>
(4) change <u>was</u> to <u>is</u>
(5) change <u>was</u> to <u>were</u>

GO ON TO LANGUAGE ARTS, WRITING, PART II.

Part II

Essay Directions and Topics

Look at the box below. In that box is your assigned topic and the letter of that topic. You must write on the assigned topic ONLY.

You will have 45 minutes to write on your assigned essay topic. If you have time remaining after you complete your essay, you may return to the multiple-choice section as long as your total time on Parts I and II does not exceed 120 minutes.

Your essay will be evaluated on its overall effectiveness based on the following features:

- Well-focused main points
- Clear organization of your ideas
- Specific development of your ideas
- Control of sentence structure, punctuation, grammar, word choice, and spelling

---

TOPIC H

Completing all the daily tasks that must be done is challenging for many people.

In your essay, describe how people might manage their daily time and tasks. Use your personal observations, experience, and knowledge to support your essay.

In preparing your essay, you should take the following steps:

- Read the **DIRECTIONS** and the **TOPIC** carefully.
- Plan your essay before you write. Use scratch paper. On the actual GED Test, these notes will be collected but not scored.
- Before you finish your essay, reread what you have written and make any changes that will improve your essay.

Your essay should be long enough to develop the topic adequately.

Answers and explanations start on page 41.

STEP 4

GED Personal Coach™

You have just finished a full-length *Practice GED Language Arts, Writing Test.* On this page and the next, you will evaluate your results and make a plan to polish up your performance for the actual test.

1. Check your answers to Part I on pages 41–43.

    -   Carefully read the explanation of each correct answer. Use this feedback to help you understand how to answer GED questions.
    -   On the chart below, circle the numbers of the questions that you answered correctly. Add the totals ACROSS for the content areas and the totals DOWN for the skills.

Content Area	Question Types			Total Correct
	Correction	**Revision**	**Construction Shift**	
Sentence Structure	5	13, 20, 30, 32, 38, 41, 48	4, 6, 14, 31, 36 45	___ out of 14
Organization	2, 7, 21, 25, 40		19, 33, 46	___ out of 8
Usage	9, 15, 16, 37, 47, 50	10, 11, 17, 18, 27, 28, 29, 39, 43, 49		___ out of 16
Mechanics	1, 8, 12, 22, 23, 24, 26, 34, 35, 42, 44	3		___ out of 12
TOTALS	___ out of 23	___ out of 18	___ out of 9	

    -   Add the Total Correct to determine how many questions you answered correctly. Write your total below.
        Total Correct ____ out of 50

2. Have your teacher read your essay and assign a score of 1, 2, 3, or 4 based on the GED Essay Scoring Guide on page 44.
    Essay Score ____

3. Use your Total Correct on Part I and your Essay Score to determine your readiness to take the actual GED Language Arts, Writing Test:

    -   If you earned a score of **2 on your essay** and **40 or more** correct <u>OR</u> if you earned a **3 or 4 on your essay** and **30 correct,** you should be ready to take the actual GED Writing Test.
    -   If you earned a score of **2 on your essay,** focus on raising your essay score. (If you earned a **1 on your essay,** ask your teacher for intensive instruction in essay writing. You CANNOT pass the GED without earning a 2 or higher on the essay.)
    -   If you earned a **3 or 4 on your essay** and got **fewer than 30 questions correct,** focus your efforts on sentence structure, organization, usage, and mechanics skills.
    -   To help you with both parts of the test, we recommend these books from New Readers Press:
        GED Scoreboost™ Essay Writing and Organization Skills
        GED Scoreboost™ Sentence Structure, Usage, and Mechanics

4. Use the *Personal Study Planner* on the next page to sharpen your approach to passing the GED Writing Test.

Personal Study Planner

Use your experience with the practice test and the evaluation chart to answer the questions.

Q: Did you answer all of the questions on Part I in 75 minutes? If not, how many questions were left?

A: _____
_____

Q: Were you able to write an essay that received a score of 3 or higher in 45 minutes? If not, what did you find to be difficult?

A: _____
_____

Q: What does your teacher say that you should improve in your essay writing?

A: _____
_____

Q: Based on your results, are you ready to take the actual GED Writing Test?

A: My score on Part I was _____. My score on Part II was _____.

I am/am not ready to take the test. (*Circle one*).

If you are ready to take the GED Writing Test, congratulations! If you are not quite ready yet, continue below.

Q: If you are not ready to take the GED Writing Test, which of the skill areas gave you the most trouble?

Look at your essay score and the evaluation chart on page 38 and check off 2 or 3 areas below. Ask your teacher to provide you with study materials that will help you to strengthen these skills.

	✓	Material Assigned	Pages	Date Finished
Sentence Structure				
Organization				
Usage				
Mechanics				
Essay Writing				

Answers and Explanations

Correction Questions, p. 5

1. **(2) replace <u>pares</u> with <u>pairs</u>** These are homonyms; they sound the same but are spelled differently. In this sentence *pairs*, which means "puts in groups of two," is needed.

2. **(1) insert a comma after <u>so</u>** Use a comma to set off an introductory word or phrase.

3. **(5) no correction is necessary** There is no error in the sentence.

4. **(2) insert <u>and</u> before <u>indicate</u>** This sentence contains a comma splice. A coordinating conjunction is needed along with the comma.

Revision Questions, p. 7

1. **(5) drywall hang** The main verb in this sentence is *hang*; it should be in the present tense and agree with the plural subject *men*. No comma is needed in the underlined portion of the sentence.

2. **(3) advantages, but it** The original sentence is a run-on. It needs a logical coordinating conjunction and a comma.

3. **(4) have caused** The verb in the original sentence is in the wrong tense. The best clue is the other verb in the same sentence, *are*, which is in the present tense.

4. **(3) prefer** The sentence has two parts that should begin with verbs in the same form: *value our relationship with you and prefer not to lose you as a tenant.*

Construction Shift Questions, p. 9

1. **(5) needs when they are trying to** The complete sentence would read, *Different people have different needs when they are trying to concentrate on challenging work.* This revision of the sentence is less wordy.

2. **(1) need the buzz of activity to focus,** The complete sentence would read, *Some people need the buzz of activity to focus, so they work well in an open area near others.*

3. **(4) Please prepare for our concert by warming up your voice at home and reviewing your music.** The words *warming* and *reviewing* both have an *-ing* ending in the correct sentence.

4. **(3) because the musicians will be tuning** The complete sentence would read, *When you enter the concert hall, please be quiet because the musicians will be tuning their instruments.* This revision of the sentence is less wordy.

Organization Questions, p. 11

1. **(3) sentence 5** There is a shift in the topic at this point. In the first four sentences, the writer comments on people's behavior. Starting at sentence 5, the writer gives advice to the reader.

2. **(5) no revision is necessary** Sentence 6 makes sense right where it is: it's the "favor" you should do for yourself.

3. **(2) remove sentence 4** This sentence is unrelated to the topic of the document.

4. **(1) A clear, fair raise policy will be followed at every level.** This sentence makes a clear topic sentence for paragraph B.

Respond to the Topic, p. 13

Check your work on each topic. Ask yourself,

☐ Did I write the topic as a question in my own words?

☐ Does my focus statement tell the main point my essay will discuss?

☐ Is my focus statement *clearly related to the topic?*

☐ Will my essay be supported with the kind of information the topic seems to ask for?

Plan Before You Write, p. 15

Check your work on each topic. Ask yourself,

☐ Did I list one supporting idea for each paragraph?

☐ Did I list details that are relevant for each supporting idea?

☐ Does each supporting idea relate to the focus and the topic?

Develop Your Support, p. 17

Check your paragraphs. Ask yourself,

☐ Does each paragraph develop one supporting idea?

☐ Does each paragraph contain specific details, examples, facts, or reasons that help convey my idea?

☐ Do the details help make the writing interesting for the readers, so they can imagine what I am explaining or describing?

Finalize Your Essay, p. 19

Check your work. Ask yourself,

☐ Do my introductions help the reader understand how my essay will address the topic?

☐ Do my conclusions relate my most important point to the topic?

☐ Have I corrected my paragraphs neatly?

In addition to checking your work on these essay topics, this is a good time to review your readiness for the GED essay overall. Think about the work you have done drafting essays for these topics, and answer the following questions:

1. Do my essays clearly respond to the prompt?

2. Are my essays clearly organized in paragraphs?

3. Do my supporting paragraphs develop one main idea?

4. Do I use details to help the reader understand my ideas?

5. What should I pay most attention to as I practice writing for the GED Essay?

6. What are my strengths as a writer? How can I use my strengths to best advantage when I write the GED Essay?

Sharpen Your Test-Taking Skills, pp. 20–21

1. **(4) insert a comma after accident** The introductory clause needs a comma after it.

2. **(3) believe** The passage is written in the present tense. Also note that the other verb in this sentence, *do notice,* is in the present tense.

3. **(1) know that their** The complete sentence would read, *In fact, experienced motorcycle riders know that their best defensive driving strategy is to assume they are invisible.*

4. **(2) join paragraphs A and B** Paragraph B helps explain the last point in Paragraph A. The two paragraphs both involve the main idea that motorcycle drivers are often not seen by other drivers.

Practice Test, Part I, pp. 28–36

1. **(5) replace there with their (Correction)** The possessive pronoun is needed, not the adverb meaning "in that place."

2. **(1) remove sentence 2 (Correction)** This sentence is not relevant to the overall topic of the article.

3. **(2) center, but (Revision)** A comma is needed before the conjunction between the two independent clauses.

4. **(5) has been established to assess (Construction Shift)** The complete sentence would read, *Now a task force has been established to assess commuters' needs across the region.* This is a clear, effective combination of the meaning of the two sentences.

5. **(4) remove to consider (Correction)** Each item in the series of options should be in parallel form. The other items are noun phrases, so the last item should be changed from a verb phrase to a noun phrase.

6. **(3) most people who stand up (Construction Shift)** The complete sentence would read, *However, the good news is that most people who stand up in front of groups and talk are scared.*

7. **(2) A good speech must have a beginning, a middle, and an end. (Correction)** This is the best topic sentence because it sums up the main point of the paragraph.

8. **(3) insert a comma after grabber (Correction)** The phrase *or strong opening* is a renaming phrase (it names the same thing as "attention grabber"). Therefore, it needs a comma before it as well as after it.

9. **(1) replace One with You (Correction)** The rest of the passage uses the pronoun *you,* so to avoid a pronoun shift to *one,* use *you* in this sentence too.

10. **(5) give (Revision)** The simple present tense verb *give* is needed in this sentence.

11. **(5) are based (Revision)** The original sentence is a fragment because it is missing part of the verb.

12. **(3) insert a comma after windows (Correction)** The introductory phrase, *To see our rates for various windows,* should be set off with a comma.

13. (3) prompt, thorough, and (Revision) The three ideas in the original sentence—*prompt, thorough, and courteous*—can be easily combined into one parallel list. This eliminates the repeated *we are.*

14. (1) your home or business to determine (Construction Shift) The complete sentence would read, *Please call if you would like me to visit your home or business to determine a price.*

15. (2) change me to I (Correction) The subject pronoun *I* is needed in this sentence.

16. (2) change agree to will agree (Correction) This action would take place in the future, so the future tense is needed.

17. (5) the crew (Revision) The pronoun is referring to the noun *crew*, which is singular. Therefore, the pronoun *they* does not match. It is better to repeat the noun for the sake of clarity.

18. (4) We do (Revision) The writer is referring to the people of his company, so the pronoun *we* should be used rather than *one,* which does not refer to any specific person or group.

19. (3) begin a new paragraph with sentence 10 (Construction Shift) A new idea begins with sentence 10: that the cleaning service will take good care of the customer's windows.

20. (2) we have carefully trained our workers (Revision) In this sentence, the introductory phrase is a dangling modifier. It isn't clear who trained the workers with the protection of the customer's windows in mind. Using the pronoun *we* emphasizes that the company trains its workers with this protection in mind.

21. (5) no revision is necessary (Correction) Sentence 12 should not be moved or deleted. It is another detail explaining how the company protects the property of the customer.

22. (4) replace you're with your (Correction) The possessive pronoun *your* is needed in this sentence, not the contraction for *you are.*

23. (3) remove the comma after you (Correction) This comma is unnecessary.

24. (4) change park to Park (Correction) This word is part of the proper noun *Rose Park.*

25. (5) move sentence 2 to follow sentence 7 (Correction) Paragraph A focuses on the public meeting, so sentence 2 does not belong there. However, it makes sense to mention the construction schedule in paragraph B, which describes some of the construction aspects of the project. Furthermore, the project schedule is mentioned in sentence 8.

26. (5) no correction is necessary (Correction) This sentence does not contain an error.

27. (4) will hear (Revision) Since this action will take place in the future, the future tense is needed.

28. (3) includes (Revision) The subject of the verb is *plan,* a singular noun, so *plan includes* is correct.

29. (2) are (Revision) The subject of the verb is *pavilions.* If you have trouble finding the subject, you can reorder the sentence like this: *Several small pavilions for group gatherings are also under consideration.*

30. (5) goods because it (Revision) The revised sentence would read, *Yeast is a vital ingredient in many types of breads and baked goods because it makes the dough fluff up and rise.* Combining these two sentences makes the text less wordy and eliminates some repeated ideas.

31. (1) they (Construction Shift) The complete sentence would read, *As the cells eat these sugars and take in oxygen, they divide and produce new yeast cells.*

32. (2) As the yeast's food supply of sugar diminishes, (Revision) The original sentence is a comma splice. By adding the word *As* at the beginning of the sentence, you create an introductory dependent clause.

33. (3) combine paragraphs C and D (Construction Shift) Paragraph D continues to describe the rising process, so it should be part of paragraph C.

34. (2) insert a comma after meetings (Correction) A comma is needed to separate items in a series.

35. (1) replace principal with principle (Correction) These are two homonyms—words that sound alike but are spelled differently and have different meanings. This sentence needs the word *principle,* meaning "an important rule."

36. (4) Call a meeting only if there is (Construction Shift) The revised sentence would read, *Call a meeting only if there is no other way to get the work done.* This is the clearest way to write the sentence.

37. (2) replace them with the agenda (Correction) The pronoun *them* does not clearly refer to any noun. It's best to repeat the noun agenda here.

38. (3) agenda. Other (Revision) The original sentence is a run-on. One way to correct a run-on is to separate it into two sentences.

39. (5) is (Revision) The passage is written in the present tense, so *is*, not *was*, is needed.

40. (4) remove sentence 11 (Correction) This sentence is not relevant to the topic of the article.

41. (5) schedule (Revision) The original sentence is a fragment because *scheduling* is not a complete verb. *Schedule* fits the present tense and matches the subject, the understood *you* (*you schedule*).

42. (5) change <u>Summer</u> to <u>summer</u> (Correction) The seasons (spring, summer, fall/autumn, winter) are not capitalized.

43. (4) feel (Revision) Note that the other verb in the sentence, *meet*, is in the present tense also.

44. (1) insert a comma after <u>meeting</u> (Correction) The introductory phrase, *As part of the meeting,* should be followed by a comma because a reader should pause there.

45. (2) responsibilities and their deadlines (Construction Shift) The complete sentence would read, *Make a note of all the participants' follow-up responsibilities and their deadlines.*

46. (3) The Traffic Department is recommending an additional traffic signal. (Construction Shift) The original topic sentence for this paragraph is too vague. This sentence specifies who is recommending the new signal.

47. (4) change <u>brung</u> to <u>brought</u> (Correction) *Brung* is incorrect English. *Brought* is an irregular past tense verb form.

48. (1) time because it (Revision) There is no error in this sentence.

49. (3) would help (Revision) The verb tense should reflect the fact that this event has not actually taken place.

50. (1) change <u>has</u> to <u>have</u> (Correction) The subject of the verb is the plural *reviews: Three previous reviews of traffic accidents. . .* The verb *have* agrees with the subject.

Practice Test, Part II, p. 37

Use the Practice Essay Review Guide on page 25 to review and evaluate your essay. If possible, work with your teacher to determine whether your essay reflects the quality of writing needed to pass the GED Writing Test.

GED Essay Scoring Guide

Characteristics by which
an essay is evaluated

	1 Inadequate	2 Marginal	3 Adequate	4 Effective
	Reader has difficulty identifying or following the writer's ideas.	Reader occasionally has difficulty understanding or following the writer's ideas.	Reader understands the writer's ideas.	Reader understands and easily follows the writer's expression of ideas.
Response to the Prompt	Attempts to address prompt but with little or no success in establishing a focus.	Addresses the prompt, though the focus may shift.	Uses the writing prompt to establish a main idea.	Presents a clearly focused main idea that addresses the prompt.
Organization	Fails to organize ideas.	Shows some evidence of an organizational plan.	Uses an identifiable organizational plan.	Establishes a clear and logical organization.
Development and Details	Demonstrates little or no development; usually lacks details or examples or presents irrelevant information.	Has some development but lacks specific details; may be limited to a listing, repetitions, or generalizations.	Has focused but occasionally uneven development; incorporates some specific detail.	Achieves coherent development with specific and relevant details and examples.
Conventions of EAE*	Exhibits minimal or no control of sentence structure and the conventions of EAE.*	Demonstrates inconsistent control of sentence structure and the conventions of EAE.	Generally controls sentence structure and the conventions of EAE.	Consistently controls sentence structure and the conventions of EAE.
Word Choice	Exhibits weak and/or inappropriate words.	Exhibits a narrow range of word choice, often including inappropriate selections.	Exhibits appropriate word choice.	Exhibits varied and precise word choice.

*Edited American English—correct usage of sentence structure, grammar, punctuation, capitalization, and spelling.

Reprinted with the permission of the GED Testing Service. © 2001 GEDTS.

Revising and Editing Checklists

Use both checklists below to improve your essay on the GED Writing Test. You can also use the editing checklist when you are answering the multiple-choice questions on Part I.

Revising Checklist

Response to the prompt

☐ Have I presented a clear focus statement in a topic sentence?
☐ Have I supplied adequate specific examples and details to support my focus statement?

Paragraphing

☐ Have I divided my supporting ideas and details into paragraphs?
☐ Does each paragraph have a clear topic and supporting sentences?

Organization of ideas

☐ Have I established a clear and logical organization?
☐ Do I have an introduction?
☐ Are all the ideas relevant—does each support the main point?
☐ Did I use a variety of short and long sentences, as well as different sentence structures?
☐ Do I have a conclusion?

Word choice

☐ Have I used a variety of words?
☐ Are the words that I have used precise and accurate?

Editing Checklist

Have I corrected sentence structure errors in these areas?

☐ Sentence fragments and run-on sentences
☐ Comma splices
☐ Improper subordination
☐ Modification
☐ Parallelism

Have I solved usage problems in these areas?

☐ Subject-verb agreement
☐ Verb form and tense errors
☐ Pronoun reference

Have I corrected mechanics mistakes in these areas?

☐ Capitalization
☐ Punctuation-commas in series, in compound sentences, with introductory elements, and with appositives; comma overuse
☐ Spelling-possessives, contractions, and homonyms

Pass the GED™ Workbooks
Five Steps to Test Success

Pass the GED Language Arts, Writing Test
Pass the GED Language Arts, Reading Test
Pass the GED Social Studies Test
Pass the GED Science Test
Pass the GED Mathematics Test

New Readers Press
Division of ProLiteracy™ Worldwide

Syracuse, New York
800-448-8878
www.newreaderspress.com

ISBN 978-1-56420-479-0

9 781564 204790